Heading North

Andrew James Murray

To a good friend Ange,

Best Wishes

Andrew J. Murray

x

NORDLAND

www.nordlandpublishing.com

Andrew James Murray

Copyright

Thanks to Derek J. Bates for the author image.

Published by Nordland Publishing 2015

ISBN E-book: 978-82-8331-010-8
ISBN Print: 978-82-8331-009-2

Andrew James Murray

DEDICATION

For Jen, always,
with love.

Andrew James Murray

CONTENTS

Foreword

I am a northern guy. I have lived the whole of my life in the north west of England. I *feel* northern. It is in my accent. It is in my attitude. It is in my preferences: my favourite season is winter, and, whenever I travel, it is to the places that both inspire and speak to me: the bleakness of the Pennines; the beauty of Cumbria; the Gothic Romanticism of Whitby; the history of Northumbria; the rugged wilderness of the Highlands; the remoteness of ancient Orkney. And, still, now, I turn my face to the north—towards Shetland and the Scandinavian countries.

I have long been interested in how other people write, holding a fascination in how they act on, or react to, inspiration. It is in this response that we enter into a dialogue with the universe. The exterior world acts as stimuli, causing a reaction in our interior world. From this process we bring something, forged in the dark of our being, out into the light. I believe this is true of all artistic people, be they poets, songwriters, painters, or novelists.

My writing is shaped by what Kenneth White termed Geopoetics. In my understanding of this, it is a way of being creative in, and being inspired by, the place where we find ourselves living. This incorporates the landscape, the natural world, the seasons, the elements, the history, the people, the mythology. *Everything*. Being present to the open world in an informed and imaginative way, having a fully-developed sense of place, on both a physical and metaphysical level.

The poems that you will find in this collection are born from this sense of place, from either the rural spaces that draw me, or the urban environment to which I am anchored. They are arranged in a deliberate order to represent a journey: a journey of both geography and time.

1

We travel from the childhood and youth of summer in the south, to the mortality-facing winter of the north. A gradual, definite route, summed up by a few lines found in one of the poems:

We ride in the wake of glaciers,
leaving behind the sunshine straits.

North, north, always north,
heading into midnight.

Andrew James Murray

Midnight, July

We writhe
with a rage to know
the unknowable,

blind to great masses
that dance in dark orbits.
And a soft, summer wind
on a night beneath stars
is no balm.

From somewhere a whistle
casts a line,

a fragile camaraderie
in a world
fell silent,

where white moth-wing
is riotous

and a spider's touch
carnal.

Fallow Beauty

Fallow beauty,
hungering to be spoiled,

possessing every glance
for a moment,

disobedient eyes
trailing her meandering mile,

a languid sway
into summer's meridian,

barelegged and barefooted,
suffused in bronze.

Wasps are persistent,
seeking out
discarded fruit,

a rotten bounty,
stripped and blackening,
putrefying
half buried in sand

alongside I,
being swallowed whole,
suddenly
breathless and old,

following a shadow
of admirable ruin.

Sea View

There is a mutual exchange,
the boats on the horizon
pass each other miles apart
but appear much closer
together.

A white-thimble lighthouse
provides scale and contrast
to the pelagic braid,

while salty notes,
redolent of summers past,
climb to this terracotta tiled balcony,
where we are reminded
that we live on an island,
perched precariously on the rim
of our outer edge,
looking out to sea.

News On A Stairwell

Sated on the stories of others,
fed in passing on casual affairs.
On stairwells, glancing,
their legible wares
are traded second hand
for faltering steps,
and behind hand murmurs
of shallow cares,
where dead unions play on,
play on, laughing.
In salacious nooks
their small town shagging
goes on, on walls,
spread everywhere.

Summer Boys

They spend fleeting moments
casting conspiratorial eyes
towards the diffident girls,
but retreat, blushing,
to their sashed gang,
with their grime-smeared marbles
and their fraternal caste.
Sat on oil stained kerbs,
harnessing the sun's fire
with jagged glass,
burning blackening holes
into paper and wood,
fed on dry grass
until blue smoke rises
—a summoned spirit,
only to be banished
when a passing parade
calls them, flying,
over stony croft.
They follow behind
in a winding line,
lost and in thrall
to the piper's call.

Parade

coveted, prime
position,
soaking up
the shade

swarming tree
wasp nest
involuntary shudder

succession of
carnival figures,
gaudy and garish

street edge
assembly
lined zombies
in mute observation

proud pensioners
festival junkies

candy floss
— death trap for flies
(a sticky end?)

exit in
anti-climax

Berlin

Hanging on the telephone
in a hazy funk.
Ice in a glass.
The words
shape-shifting silver bream,
occasionally
catching the light.

The ice shifts,
tying me down,
caught on a line
encumbered, turbid.
Tasting Berlin: Berlin,
diluted,
hanging on the telephone
in a hazy funk.

Old Town

1.
As is their wont,
the ancestors speak of nothing,

just leave their handprints
on rock, drying in shadow.

In sterile dust
we kick
careless trails,

tracks opening up
in animal minds.

In towns
we lay our markers down,

watering holes
within arid charms.

The rats have our number,
wait us out,

sandstorms filling our lungs
like egg timers.

2.
On the porch
she reads Capote.
Turns her face to the south.

Her bookmark is an old photograph
of an old man; a girl; a dog:
'Mary and her grandfather Jasper, around 1900'.
He: sat, stern and saturnine, wearing the dust.
She: stood, hand lightly on his shoulder,
glaring at the camera,
facing down posterity:
Not yet. Not yet.

The dog is unnamed.
The birdcage in the window, empty.
In the book there are voices on the wind.
Here, just the parched whisper
of turned vellum.

Sunflower

The sunflower
grows alone,
and tall,

attaining a dominance
and a penchant
for flattery.

In Spanish Hills

In this fiery furnace
is forged a languid blade,
yet in these hills
is a vibrant pulse.
And formed within
this small enclave
is a definite sense
of them, and us.

The eye drowns in colour
and shimmering haze,
yet we carry around
a windswept moor.
On an azure calm
our vision sails,
but what comes to mind
is a battered shore.

The House Sleeps

Silent but for a clock, ticking.

The children are lost
in raiment
and unfathomable furrows
of thought.

Walls bleed resin
of joy and sorrow.

The house sighs deeply
—first gasp of the newborn.

Outside life goes on,
with a dirge;
an elegy;
a mournful song

in the cycle of the butterfly
and all creaturely keening.

The house is silent,
but the garden sings.

The sun lowers
like a casket.

Bright Garden

Overfilled, flirting, fragrant swathes,
beds of deliberating bees
in the yellows, purples, reds.

The youths lazy
in their skittish, coquettish games,
all sweat shine and rosy,
cotton grass stained.

In summer's last hurrah,
green metallic flies,
gathering in their end of days,
are chased away by a young girl's
high red-brick wall saunters.
The boys look up,
all nudges and sniggers,
and the breeze comes from the future,
nostalgic and vague.

On A Train

Window the eye
to fleeting worlds.

Silver birch
and scrubland.
Contours of
the cultivated man.

Smokestacks.
Steel tracks.

Copper corroded
blood stains.

Diesel plumes
caught in
conflicting winds,

twisting amorphous
trails.

We bleed our desire
in profusion,
fleeing our
structured hives.

Rushing headlong
to the end of the line.

Low River

Listless and limp;
unmoving bowers,

no rain to wash
her barren banks

or call to arms
redundant
birds,

incumbent on
unforgiving
scree.

A hiker
slides
an angled
drop,

picks a route
along
the exposed spine,

leaves behind
dislodged stones.

Andrew James Murray

From A Clifftop

My vision descends upon rebuffed passes,
crest falling upon a cast of thousands

the oystercatcher,
   daring me to laugh
    at its slapstick bill
    and solemn pose;
    self-deprecating stance

the cormorant,
    sat upon its nonchalant throne,
    satin silhouette
    curling away like cigarette smoke

the turnstone; the redshank,
    dining companions
    on the fraying edge
    of an argent infinity

beating away in habitual hunger,
mocking me in my partial decline.

Ochre skies burn obsidian ashes,
a sudden burst driving stakes to the sand.

Dark, distant smudges
waiver

beyond voice; beyond influence,
merge into the broad strokes
of a spreading shadow,
a fast frame sequence
engulfing reason, mood.

Ocean

With an ardent longing,
sending her mating call over corpulent dune
to my sand-sprinkled raptures,
wildly adoring
her untameable passion
but knowing my place;

walking these ravaged islands,
carrying the frantic coupling
in my bedchamber,
alone,

tasting the salty spume still,
her lingering kisses
an invitation
to slip beneath her surface,
sighing.

Canary Wharf, Morning

Sunrise over angled skies.
Reflected light on
glass and steel.

Still water shine
and strengthening hum
of time-fixated
suited drones,

speed induced and web infused.
See the parade
of passive martyrs.

One day, maybe,
just one day,
sit and watch the world go by.

When Camping, Lost

Run away, run away,
the silted stream follows her way,

and the bedraggled bunch
look for landmarks
along her unfamiliar bends.

The sky is leprous
through leafed fingers,
mottled and thick
like porridge.

Crouching shrubs,
poised to pounce,
invigilate
their anxious pass,
as the forest withdraws
her benevolent cowl,
her regional tongue
breaking out
into the maniacal chatter
of startled birds.

Shadows condense
in a sea of fronds,

the ground breathing in
scented mosses and rain,
running through the ground in veins.

Ynys Môn

A vast, star-sprayed night
and a sombre ocean
diminishes us
in their dark entirety.

Druidic ghosts,
in the destruction
of their sacred groves,
linger lost, in rocky coves.

Sharp teeth — a granite snarl,
snap at our unsteady tread.
A salivary film
breaks our nerve,
and we fall back, yellow,
upon the seeming surety of sand.

We strain against the blackness,
reaching out for worlds
on the edge of forever.
To lights burning
beyond sky and foam.

To infinity, rising.

Seafront

It smells like a Manchester bus stop;
of piss, and chips,
the accumulated detritus
gathering in the corners
like the unclaimed ashes
of disregarded deceased.

Deck chairs and windbreaks
hibernate
beneath the tied shrouds
of bulging, unshapely tarpaulins.

The beach is swept clear
by jarring, unimpeded gusts
competing with the cutting cry
of rapacious raptors
and cocksure gulls,
settling for a life of stale scraps
on the concrete, calling.

A marginalising, unmanned
Antonine wall,
its faltering facade of flaking paint
testifies to a trading of blows,
accepting the rain and abandonment
with a certitude of faith.

It is as though every vital aspect,
all *dynamic,*
has been gathered up
and deposited elsewhere.
Some coloured other place,

23

where children's laughter
drowns out the birds,
and pensioners peer out to sea
with sun blind eyes.

Grey Heron On The School-Run

A still, distant wisp,
delineation of poise,
holds its ambivalence
out of the reach of eager children.

On its floating midden
it remains unattainable,
while the geese,
raucous and molesting,
have left their mess
out in the fields,
hidden in the grass
for unsuspecting feet.

The bell measures out the day,
divided into parts,
and there is a hurrying
at the last
— a harrying of stragglers,
as the river converges
into a bottleneck of receptivity,
a porosity of parts
not yet slaves to notifications.

Will these days be remembered,
I wonder,
in the final moments?

The Sun Stays High

A breeze gets up amid placid dreams,
attracting the eyes of languid hosts.
The sudden movement draws them out.

An old man wilts like a flower,
his strength sapped by countless summers.
His skin taut, tanned leather.

The children play on, reddened rogues,
among the scrub, with salted lips.
Shaded by their ceaseless scorn.

Wooden wind chimes, glockenspiels,
induce a torpid, cloaking down.
The sun stays high, consolidates.

Sky

I am yet to be convinced
there exists anything more wondrous
than the sky;
whether clouding or blue,
an all-encompassing
overview of heaven.

Reflected in still water.
As above, so below.
A shimmering symmetry.
And I, trapped within these elements,
forged in fire,
arms stretched upwards,
fingers splayed,
always, always,
falling short.

Backyard

Cold flagstone, washed
and swept clean,
potted geraniums and foxgloves
struggling to climb in scarce sunlight.
A neighbour
peers over the wall, on tiptoes,
comparing and contrasting
minimal squares
in linear cells of shadow.

A brief glimpse of a swift,
sleeping on the wing,
suddenly there then gone
— connections cut before the heart
can rise to find substance
in coloured heights,
anchored still
as it is
to circadian greys.

Muse

In the act
of refining
she is raped
of her raw
allure.

In our ascension
to lust
we exalt her.

Storm Coming

They said a storm was coming,
and not a moment too soon.
The garden drinks thirstily,
the birds, shaken from their roosts,

ride in advance,
their cloaked consorts,
robed in capes
of jackdaw feathers,

swooping first over parched soil
and shrivelled roots,
twisted beneath uniform,
country lane hedgerows.

A woman stands at the window,
flinching every time
the current finds voice.

She loses her nerve
and battens down.
The windows rattle
like a dead man's bones.

She is an ogham script,
read from bottom to top.
In the scattered ash,
a dog howls, lost.

These Hills I Know

A shot-burst
of starling
startles the eye,

and simultaneous
searing staccato,

nearing and receding
with every arc,

then falling upon the land
like a shadow;
like a plague.

These hills I know
through my ancestral blood,

coursing along my
second hand veins.

The contours I see
with my reconstructed eye,

bequeathed by those
in whose image I was made

without a thought
for that next blank page.

Twilight

Twilight is a truly mystical time.
To taste the sublime;
feel the caress;
first undress
the senses.

Dockyard

Discharged of duty,
the cranes are extinct sauropods,
fossilising as they stand.
Smudges of smoke
and a clattering of rain
on corrugated iron
fill the night.

Caulkers and other men
of toil,
circumscribed by whistle
and clock,
are gone,

having filed by
the oil-black water
a final time,

the women's
failed crane bags
and grimoires
flung into the inky depths.

The tone
is commensurate with the hour,
drifting, reconciled,
on a cat's-paw
breeze,

as the pub empties
on the moated hill,
wistful eyes

riding the inlet down
to the padlocked gates,
before turning and blurring
against the torrent,
— hard and warm
and cauterising.

A Gentle Wind

A gentle wind
sifts through
a gathering
of leaves

turns yellowing
pages
of discarded
tenets

tousles the mane
of troubadours

caresses the cheek
of cowards.

Woman In A Cafè

There is a woman in a cafè in Manchester,
who pines for old Ancoats.
She rambles about extinct
buildings she could never have seen,
latte moustached and leary,
tongue flicking over cracked lips
between each soiled ode.
Her fingerless mittened hands
clutch bunched plastic bags
proprietorially
as she rises,
swinging them in an arc
through an avalanche of sugar and salt.

She steps out of the door
and bumps into barrow boys;
refuses the wares of hawkers;
dodges the belt buckle jousts
of Jersey Boys and Bengal Tigers
in their choreographed clashes.

Her shuffling feet,
on cobbled roads,
scuff the scuttlers'
territorial lines,
as she heads off towards the canal,
riven by vagary,
seeing gaslights,
smog,
but not the car.

Two worlds converge,
suddenly,
then dissipates.

Gone Confessions

The echo of gone confessions,
sounding among dancers
unable to dance.
The sorrow of lovers
unable to kiss,
without the prying eyes
of hindsight.

On the midnight lawn,
weeping willow limbs
take the tendril shape
of figures remembered
on balmy nights,
before the dawn emerged cold
and ivory white,
echoing on, and on, and on.

Detour

Down by the river side,
below a bridge of broken bottles.
Hearts tug on the sleeve.
A cold corrosion settles in.

Gleaming cats' eyes in ragged lines.
Dogs bark unheeded fate
into the night.

The obituaries
of blown newspaper pages
clamour for one last chance
to be framed by living breath
in a retreating world,

rolling away up
a steep embankment
of spilled seed
and lacerated sheathes.

Slattocks Canal

The sedentary
figure of a fisherman
by the redundant waterway.

Still nothing has he caught.
Could it be he's been out-thought
by such a tiny brained foe?
— He doesn't think so.

Beneath the carpet
of conquering weeds,
between the barbs
of needle-reeds,
their number is smaller;
the water shallower,
and strategically placed
shopping trolleys,
half-submerged,
contribute to the clogging
of this coagulated artery.

A train thunders past,
the fisherman shifts,
night drifts in, reluctant.

Wolf River Blues

(On The Death Of Jeff Buckley)

I lie on my back and watch the sky,
much as I did in childhood;
it is the same.

Back flat to the earth,
a dowsing rod of bone,
feet pointing to the sibilant stream

whilst my head swirls in muddier waters,
silted eyes glimpsing
an extinguishing light,
sinking fully clothed
in a twisting, vanishing
undercurrent,

then rising
bloated and booted
to a new sun
burning away insignificant truth,

to hang his wrung out carcass
to dry
and be remoulded to taste.

And a Memphis elegy
for our inarticulate hour,
one final, slow song
to make love to,
like it may be our last time.

Pumpkin

a hollowed out,
    rictus grin
    placed prominently
    at this liminal time

a curious crossroads
    of old and new
    with but a cursory nod
    to the peaceful host

frail shelter
    from this Samhain storm
    a rail of russet leaves
    and borne
    the broken limbs
    of oak

and scorned
    a single flame,
    faltering.

Andrew James Murray

No Jubilee Flags

The last time he was here was in '77,
jubilee flags strung around the square
from lamppost to lamppost,
a fluttering, captured, prism of sky,
kerbstones painted intermittently
red-white-blue, red-white-blue,
a tessellated mandala, preserving all.

A piano was rolled out of one of the houses,
cumbersome, out of tune,
discordant, still,
on the decades-old breeze.

The passage is still there,
leading behind the houses to the sandhills,
where ghost stories were told
as the sun slipped behind
the undulating mounds,
badger setts swallowing the eye
in their impenetrable thresholds of jet.

Seconded in the shrubbery
he sees a mattress; boards;
whittled sticks in the ground
staking out an elliptical border,
and feels a sudden gratification
that a new generation
are reoccupying his old dens,
Saxons on Roman ramparts;
faceless inheritors of place.

Requiting, he departs,

for the final time,
taking something with him,
leaving a little behind.

Andrew James Murray

Ode To The Unborn

And so was born an impersonal love,
whilst I was still learning
of the idea in its abstract,

you was already fading,

ebbing away
into a bloody tomorrow
(the crimson stream
seeping into sandbagged hope,)

and we, helpless against
the body's machinations,
left to wonder about *everything,*
making taboo all championed names,
as we fell further away
from the finishing line.

Sailing To Wemyss Bay

Heading into the rain
we catch our breath
at an ephemeral hint
of mainland,

a crosswind of coalescence
defining faint lines,
low cloud rolling back
over the hills,
drawing us in.

The water, the sky,
a uniform grey,
draining the pastel boards of artists,
with a cold that worms its way
through our layered skins.

A wayward lock of hair,
protruding,
tugs like the label of her hat.
A salinity of sorrow
— spindrift and tears,
merges on the crucible of her face.

As we come in
the landscape, the heartscape,
finds definition.
Rain licks
like an ecstatic tongue.

Spider Webs

A paucity of lines
to begin with,

held by examples
of faith
unattached
to a creed,

forming into white,
frosted webs,
rising to be
a tangle of sky,

prone to bead
on dew-dusted mornings,

each tremulous
strand

born of hunger
and longing.

Jen

Hair like a
    tiger's eye
Bands that shine
    in autumn light
A longing carves within
    the heart
What the eye seizes
    in delight

An innocence denies
    the stars
Of whom the heavens
    first laid claim
The mind recreates
    a face
Lips whisper at
    a name

Andrew James Murray

Words On A Bridge

I remember reading of a Parisian bridge,
the Pont des Arts,
sagging beneath the weight
of padlocked pledges,
her barnacled palisades
dipping to drink from the Seine.

This bridge, here, a lesser cousin,
sun lighting on her slender nape,
is festooned with words,
the variable lines of scribes
in marker and pen.
Amidst the patchwork
of diatribe and devotion,
my eye is drawn to a post-it note,
stuck dead centre:

poetry is when
the language of the soul
escapes into
the common tongue

I thought it pretentious.

I moved on to read the other lines,
but my eyes kept returning
to that fading, yellow slip,
a stanza of disparity
surrounded by stiff banalities
and wilting vulgarities.

poetry is when
the language of the soul

48

escapes into
the common tongue

Just who was the bard of this bridge,
paying a toll in words
of thrift?

I fished out a pen, then,
suddenly aware of an approaching woman,
plunged it back
into the sanctuary of my pocket.
But, nailing me with a half-cocked smile,
she uttered a single word
as she passed me by:
"Contribute."

I imagined her then the poetess,
both collaborator and muse,
planting a seed and moving on,
the hem of her trench coat
flapping around her legs
in the river wind.

Gargoyles

The figures loom high above us, beneath spires, tall
Silent witnesses to the predilections of flesh
Perched firmly upon rain-lashed, sandstone walls
Weathered and worn, writhing in still form
Kissed by the sun and the moon's fingering frost
The winds of the north with their finite call
Have taken their hoary toll, and time, always time,
Burrowing her way from the inside out
Her threaded veins spreading their minute crawl
Yet impervious still, they cling on, strong,
Obstinately, impertinently, outliving us all

Blackbird

Songstress of the twilight
that follows your flight.
I am lost in your song;
on the dark of your wing.
Awash and away
from pale, new beginnings.

You lead in your dance
of shadow and light,
in the time-between-time
you call into being.
We straddle the threshold
of worlds, you and I.

Foreseeing each birth
and all endings.

Sunday Elegy

1.
What auguries visited us, undivined?
When fate's footfalls
arrived without echo.

Elders huddle
in shadows of faltering light.

We bear the weight
of the fallen
to the hills,
tears half glimpsed
in torchlight.

Imploring Deity,
gripped by forgotten
vulnerabilities,
our fragile images
shattered to their juvenile core.

Children of dust,
our time an eye-blink
in eternity,
we seek one moment
of reconnection.
Striving to rise
from the killing fields,
we turn our face to the stars.

2.
Leisurely morning.
Sunday driving.

Wildflower meadowland.
Give me an untamed corner
to rest my head beneath the sky.
A grassy bed
for you and I.

A chance to reveal
my true self.
Humbled in my undress.
Ogle my bared,
naked soul.
Inhale this fragrant
wilderness.

All the week
should be a Sunday.
Recounting pastoral poems
and idyllic dreams.
Exploring eerily familiar landscapes.
Painting portraits of
recurring themes.

Sentinel windmills
along the coastline.
Polluting nothing
but the skyline.

Gulls cry forlorn
over empty shores.

The searching eye
yearns for peopled towns,

where scavengers may gorge
upon easy pickings

and the relentless tide
of swarming masses

conspire to hide
the fallen down.

3.
The sudden, demented
scream of a gull.

Midnight murder.

Iridescent ocean.

Glittering
diamond hoard.

Never giving up
its secrets,

it gives to me
wonder

and sickness.

Lighted Candles

Lighted candles.
Burning incense.
Setting the mood
for words.
Simple invocation.

Tapping at the window.
Airborne leaves.
Seeking shelter
to nestle
and quietly rot.

The flickering flames
draw to themselves
sleep,
like moths, burning
in their deadly
attraction.

Northern Girl

born in rain
raised on the northern wind

scattered over
blackstone moor

the smell of dusk
and crowberry in her hair

head cushioned
by cotton grass, bracken

the twite whispers
in her ear

eyes suggest
the circling merlin

accustomed to
feel

peat water
bleed

dissolution
on the Pennine ridge

Prague, Late November

1.
A crystal cold
falls sharp
upon the city of towers,

upon the Jewish remnants
of an age-old struggle,
keeling and succumbing
in the dawn and the dusk.

Hurdling prostrate beggars
we bridge the rolling river,
crawling for solace
to our procured holes,
tasting the cuisine
with the blood and the dust.

2.
Hotel room.
Condensing copulations
form rivulets
upon the muffling pane.
In the slanted light,
dust motes dance,
erratic.

Radiators splutter into life,
and the storytellers weave their words.
Dylan sings of Sara, *to* Sara,
pouring his soul into his *other*,
forever bleeding her forsaking of him

on shuffle.

I watch mine,
watch her walk
in soft imagining,
unaware of her nakedness,
passing in and out of shadow,
in any room;
any city,
entwined in our fate.
Outside, sirens.

3.
A day trip devoid of laughter,
we slip into the slipstream
of silent newsreel,
fingering a death mask
of macabre attraction.
Terezín,
cold, cold, Terezín,
bequeathed to the aged
in their mirroring decay.
To fade away together
beneath the ghost
of a fostered despair,
and the terrible, terrible certainty,
of God's impotence.

Raw Mojo

The bleak, blushes of dusk. A Highland wind
licks at a heart, wrapped in leaves.
Buried beneath a pine cone, needles.

Drink 'til I can drink no more;
just watch the dead
impose in plagues.

A girl, dark, unfamiliar,
dares to draw the focus
of these phantom scarred eyes,
blood rushing in her alluring anonymity.

A taste of ash, I eat my father.
I am an amalgamation
of anecdote and mannerism.
Assimilated slow and left to boil.

Magisterial day. Insouciant night.
Sin suggests an arbitrator.
I need a new translation,
from the prophet's native tongue.

Two Brothers

Night falls fast
to my latticed eyes,

black tar flowing over
unsullied plumes
condemned to crave a mirage,

fluttering in a contained fury,
and I see the grace of angels.

In the space between words
glides a spectre,
encircling our gathered wagons,

looking for a way in.

A smokescreen of words
is our stockade,

a reluctance to breathe new life
into old ghosts,
fading in the firelight.

His face, always grave,
lengthens,
becomes lupine.

I reach for the family silver.

The Invisible Hills

We are boundered
by invisible hills,

nestling us
in our calm delusions.

Birds ride the lines of our electric lives.

On softly dissolving cobwebs
thoughts escape,
circumnavigate the globe,

reach those in exile
still going insane
in their own particular way.

When you live in a small town
you often encounter
your own ghost,

anchored to decaying landscapes,
pursuing outgrown pleasures
that then were everything.

Young drones
plugged into the swarm,
hovering in their fluorescent thrall,
awaken only once
to the light brushing of her skin, paled,

and desire
to take her writhing in their arms,
biting hard.

In carved hollows,
shaven skulls regress
to a common ancestor.

Painted ladies hide behind
reputable smiles.

An occasional breath
sweeps over those breasts,
and briefly she moves amongst us,
manifest,
but the mortal eye is fixed on stone.

Through pavement cracks,
pores in the skin,
her scent seeps,

mingles with the moribund
in their stark denial,
walled within a wail
of settling,

in charnel houses
of convoluted charm.

Reeds

It is not
   the way
the reeds
   move in
the wind

but the way
   the wind
moves
   the reeds

No More

No more. No more bleaching white
the nicotine stained flesh
of your fingers,
picking at the sterile
veneer of cordiality
amidst the well-thumbed
scattered deserts
from which ruins strive to rise.

No more counting down the markers,
elbows jostling territorially,
courting, sequential swans
rising in toasts, triumphant.
Your slow, inexorable withdrawal
left behind a vacuum,
the equilibrium of a table
out of kilter.

No longer the trumpeted parading
of the heir apparent,
the tedious repetition
of vine and tongue,
reproduced seasoned lines
framing the true inheritance
and held to likeness.
Casual comparity no more. No more.

Canticle

Over the hilltops,
the north acts as cantor,
singing a canticle of ice
over conceding land.

It submits passively,
turning rigid
as the descant
descends.

In these frozen shores
all colour withdraws,
except a waxwing-flush
irruption.
This tender thread,
(Icelandic bred),
unravels south,
in hunger.

New Year, Morning

Half the world is hurting,
turning its face to shadow.
Moldering moments,
kindle to flame,
are undefined images,
lost to a cold,
northwesterly wind,
licking at the edges
where the numbness fades.

Firs stand conspicuous
among their naked cousins,
all tendenous needles
and cadaverous cones.

The sky is leaden.
The streets are all
unchartered lanes.

An unknown bird calls out
this new day; this new year.

Everything is redeemable.

St.Mary's Snows

Christ on the cross
in a swirling maelstrom.

Nuns
whirling dervishes
spinning immaculate,
washing line
robes,

gathering up blind children
in night's under-wing,
talons flexed,
stripping veiling rags
from the bright
assailant.

Wild revenants flee
the howling smoke rings
of dilating eyes,

quickly absolving me
of my mundanity
in this Roman Catholic reverie.

Suddenly, suddenly.

Laments Of The Urban Dead

They die a slow death,
as a matter of routine.

Wasting away out of habit.

We bind ourselves to each other
with unwritten contracts,

suffering the banality
with a sense of duty.

Man is a social creature.
Long has the hermit
provoked tales of eccentricity
and scorn.

Merlin in the wildwood,
driven insane by slaughter.

The washer at the ford.
The bloody water.

Degenerate, industrial town,
crumbling
in your aged decay,

your impoverished veins,
your arrested heart,
has spawned
a thousand broken souls,
condemned to haunt
your desolate roads.

Broken dreams;
broken stones,
hungry to claim
broken bones.

Living wraiths lament
their atrophying tombs,
wailing behind
the nailed boards.

January rain
is cold, and hard,

driven, angled arrows
pierce our casual armour.

Dark the festival
aftermath,

we seek shelter
in our burrows,
nestling instinctively
in our vacuous hangover.

We condense ourselves
into these cancerous nests,

despair soon festering
among the jostling forms,

eating away
at hope;
at joy,

and anything of real significance.

The haunting faint strains
of a sad lament.

She is still resplendent
in her beautiful grief.

An after-glow framing her
in the interring dusk,

a brightness enhancing
her dignified despair.

A still silhouette,
caught in paralysis.

My head is heavy
with the burden
of a portentous dream.

She turns to try and solicit a smile.
With her torn face,
her bleeding eyes.

The clouds are corpulent
devourers of vision,

insisting limitation
to the ardent eye.

Their indolent drift
denies the heavens
in their profundity.

I am clay,
made of stardust;
made of stars.

Crows

A disheartening of crows
gathered in winter fields.

Naked trees
from disused rail road tracks,

dark stains
on white linen.

In trust we are led
through this stark terrain,

senses soaked
in sparse liquor,

a hungry air tasting our flesh,

a murmuring
of hardened, thirsting
soil.

They rise, wheeling,
across the sky,

black flecks of mortality
in widening whites of eyes.

Savage Sky

In this savage sky,
in this ragged hour,
a low, winter sun
glazes soft
all flesh of inordinate pallor,
embarrassed by impotence.

Unravelling powder blue ribbons,
colouring brittle braids
blown among briered
mountains of white.
Black cattle bellowing
in coarse vernacular
a dumb language of instinct, lust.

And crying like a child, each insipid sow.

You can smell the sea,
but not see it,
cupped in hands of granite,
cold, loved.
Suffering the separation
of centuries, more.

Andrew James Murray

And Now The Winter

And now the winter.
A sentence imposed
for the summer's sins.
The trees,
dead, deformed giants,
with skeletal limbs,
standing steadfast
against the biting wind.
A gnarled, livid claw
beckons us on through
Glencoe's slaughtered air.

Blowing vapoured breath
onto stiff fingers, haunted lips
recalling the scented taste
of ribboned lungs,
the eye is lost in a blue-tinged sweep
of a landscape
where Canada Geese move,
and nothing besides.

Absolved of casual highs,
and lethargies in sullen snows,
we ride in the wake of glaciers,
leaving behind the sunshine straits.

North, north, always north,
heading into midnight.

Stromness

A solitary road, cobbled, winding,
shaking off a ginnel here, a square there.
Engineered, perhaps, to break the tumult
of wind and sea. Wearing its blue plaques
upon a proud, trench coat sleeve.

Does this blonde
hold Norse secrets in her heart?
Does that old man
tap out the route of smugglers' tunnels?
Both circle each other with a complicit knowing,
while I stand out like a sore thumb,
dressed to go whaling,
or discover the North Passage.

A peregrinating, prehistoric hulk
cleaves in two the liquid dark.
Yellow jacket wasps work the night,
observed from a draughty window,
partially obscured by the frenzied throes
of a tattered, Scottish flag,
straining at the leash to be free.

Walkers On Brodgar, December

The wind brings a judgement.
Sheltered on the lea side,
casting lots
in their wounded number,
they hang low in

the grass beyond the stones,
fallen back and hardy,
swaying in
fractured shafts
of meagre light.

Their splintered line leads back
towards Stenness,
and cold, silver Harray,
mirroring the suspended sky
and aerial arc
of sky pirates.

Time is enchambered,
a mummified captive.
The early dusk hesitates,
reluctant to pass
where everything is numbered
in gravity and guesswork,

even these men,
here, waiting,
ciphers as they are,
of tooth and bone.

A Dream

A recital in sleep:
  "The long boats were
    narrow, swift knives, slicing through butter."

We fell ashore and poured into our moulds.

Pavement cafés in Paris.

A bearded colossus playing cards
with a blind, black man,
who sneaks a glance at the giant's hand from behind
dark glasses
when left alone.

Morrison fleeing his own obese monster,
striving vainly for anonymity.

  "I longed to sleep
    in soft, suffocating snow, slowly melting
      in sunlight, like the words of a dream upon
        waking."

Greenland Sharks

They glide blind
beneath the ice,

parasites attached to their eyes
like waving tassels,
devouring sight.

The stuff of nightmares,
closed off to light,
they remain sealed within
this frozen womb

beneath the Inuit, who,
in their feathered tongue,
sing to the birds
of a woman, old,

whose urine-soaked rag,
snatched into the sea
on careless gusts,

shifts into Skalugsuak
— mother of sharks,

while snowdrift smoors
their unseen world,
conceals their languid,
toxic, pass.

Three Poems In Stockholm

1.
Anchored mists hold down
the grey waters
of Saltsjön.

The mournful baritone
of a foghorn
splinters the hull,
grinds the bones,
raises us up
from our slumbering
wooden berth,

to climb high above
the city's fitful dreams.

In Södermalm,
shining in a multicoloured,
chequered dress,
a girl breezes along with an armful
of sunflowers,
creating a fissure of brightness
in the milky gloom,
ploughing a passage of light
right through to
the warm facades of Gamla Stan.
Blind to all else,
we follow her down.
2.
Mozart plays

in a culinary crypt,
candlelit quiche
and obligatory coffee
on rustic tables.

In the corners
dwell the passive Vikings,
eyeing us tourists
in our centred squalls
of confusion,
a staccato chatter
climbing the bare bricked walls,
spreading out along the arches
of the cavernous chamber
far beneath the narrow streets
pounded by traders
of all nations,
exchanging silver for amber;
copper for jet.
I could stay here forever,
always with a book,
hidden away from life
and time's parade,
disturbing the dogs
with insensible words.

3.
Sunday Stockholm.
The rain reminds me
of home.

Through the inner archipelago:

figures on the bridge
watch the wake
of our land-launched thirsts,
as we drink the dregs
of the Baltic Sea,
until our figure of eight
brings us about,
still outside on the deck
and exposed to the cold.
The figures have gone,
scourged and scattered
by the icy wind,
but two sea eagles
are there,
surveying our
laboured return
from their spindly haunts.

She Sings

She sings low,
in Swedish,

layering the already
laden air.

Rain, soft and insistent
against the window.

Sunk deep in leather,
I rain from the inside out.

The clock freezes
at midnight,

winnowing decades, moments,
heartbeats.

This groove-caught,
vinyl ghost
ploughs a lonely furrow,

her repeated
time-locked echoes

stir my viscid
black tar heart.

Jag var så kär.
Jag var så kär.

Words Unmet

There are words
unmet,
never heard,
but are carved
on the heart,
like runes.

She wrote a poem,
a three-line haiku.
Scratched it
onto the surface
of a large pebble
and threw it into the sea.

Gave it back.

Andrew James Murray

Acknowledgments

Thanks to: my parents, Fred and Lilian, for the great start, my wife Jen for keeping me grounded, my children Shannon, Courtney, Millie and James for keeping me young, the team at Nordland Publishing for their vision, and everybody else along the way.

Midnight July has appeared in Best of Manchester Poets
Ynys Môn has appeared in The Ugly Tree
Sunflower and an alternate version of *Pumpkin* have appeared in What The Dickens?
St.Mary's Snows has appeared in The Folk On The Hill

Andrew James Murray

About the author

Andrew James Murray was born in 1971, and remains firmly rooted in his childhood town, in Manchester, England. He is married and has four children. Among other things, he has worked as a postman, a foster carer, and a volunteer youth mentor. His poetry has appeared in various anthologies and publications, including Best Of Manchester Poets. He has both a poem and a short story in The Northlore Series–Folklore, and is the second poet to be published in the Songs of the North Series.

He can be found at cityjackdaw.wordpress.com

Andrew James Murray

NORDLAND PUBLISHING

Follow the North Road.

nordlandpublishing.com
facebook.com/nordlandpublishing
Nordlandpublishing.tumblr.com

www.nordlandpublishing.com